Message from Angelo
To All People on this Planet

Angelo, the Angel Cat, Speaks
on Behalf of all Beings of the
Animal Kingdom on this Planet

By Aurelia Louise Jones

Mount Shasta Light Publishing
PO Box 1509
Mount Shasta, CA 96067-1509
www.mslpublishing.com

Angelo's Message
Angelo, the Angel Cat,
Speaks To All People on this Planet

Copyright © 1999, 2000 by Aurelia Louise Jones
Copyright © 2009, 2012, 2015 Victoria Lee
Mount Shasta Light Publishing
All Rights Reserved

Portions of this publication may only be reproduced with the
written permission of the publisher. Name of the author and
publisher must be included on any reproduced material. A copy
must be sent to the publisher for approval.

First Edition, March 1999
Second Edition, May 2000
Third Edition, July 2012
Fourth Edition November 2015
Printed and bound by United Graphics, Inc., U.S.A.

ISBN: 978-0-9823229-2-5

2012 Edition Designed by Silverlining Designs

Published by Mount Shasta Light Publishing
P.O. Box 1509
Mount Shasta, CA 96067-1509
mslpublishing.com

Tribute to Mother Earth

Oh! Mother, my tears
fall upon your face.
I just remembered.....
We, the Lightworkers
have returned.....
To spread our Web
of Love around you.

From distant stars
and galaxies,
From lives past, present and future,
We come to guide your healing.
We, the Lightworkers, one soul to another,
Touch the hearts of many each day.
With each recognition, we laugh, smile and cry.
Our Love is abundant, flowing, shimmering.

We, the Lightworkers, in perfect joy
Quietly expand Unconditional Love.
Spin now ever so gently as you warm yourself,
For we, the Lightworkers are back
From eons behind and ahead.
May Love, Laughter and Tears of Joy
Rain now and forever more upon your face.

—Author unknown, Thank You for the Prayer!

Table of Contents

Tribute to Mother Earth iii
Dedication. v

CHAPTER 1
Introduction by Angelo 1
Animals' Purposes. 5
Animal Kingdoms 7

CHAPTER 2
Important Message from Angelo and Tender-Heart 13
Farm Animals 15
Animals Have Equal Rights 20

CHAPTER 3
Animals Are Not "Disposable" 27
Animal Experiments in Research 29
Abandoned Animals 32
Just a Cat?.. 35

CHAPTER 4
Young Animals and Children 39
Pet Shops. 44
Domestic Animals 48
The Slaughter of Horses 48
Imitate The Native People 51
Animals in Rodeos 54
Animals in Zoos and The Circus. 54

CHAPTER 5
Let My People Go 57
The Biggest Secret! 64
Angelo's Conclusion 67

CHAPTER 6
Message from Adama, The High Priest of Telos. 71
Let There Be Peace on Earth. 79
Prayer for Animals. 80
Suggested Reading 82
Angelo's Mission. 84
Mt. Shasta Publishing Publications. 86
Publisher's Note 88

Dedication

Angelo's Message
For the Victory of Love!

I, ANGELO, and my dear feline friend, Tender-Heart, are dedicating this message to the "Victory of Love and Compassion" for all animals on this planet. We know that the day humanity has enough wisdom, compassion and love to stop hurting animals in any way, shape or form will also be the day when humans will come to know their own glorious victory in God. It will be the day when all Creation will remember their Divinity and the Heavens will open wide.

On that victorious day, we will all begin to share this planet "equally" in a Great Brotherhood of Love. Humans will then come to perceive the animal kingdom from a higher perspective and realize the great part we have played in helping human evolution at the cost of so much suffering from our kingdom. We have tolerated much abuse for hundreds of thousands of years because of our great love for you. We have kept incarnating again and again, never knowing the fate we would have to endure.

We also want to bestow our great appreciation to all those humans who, so relentlessly and faithfully, champion the rights and welfare of animals. We thank the Earth Mother for hosting us with so much love and tolerance. We express our deep gratitude to Her for providing all of us, humans and animals alike, the platform we need for our evolutionary process.

Know that those who are relentlessly toiling for the ethical treatment of animals on this planet, and who stand guard as their protectors, are loved and treasured beyond measure by millions of beings from the animal and angelic kingdoms in many galaxies, planets and dimensions. You will soon reap a great reward.

We, the Beings of the Animal Kingdom, all join together to offer the fruit of the immense burden and suffering we have carried on this planet through the long ages of Earth's evolution and dedicate it to the Victory of Love and Compassion among all Sentient Beings.

We also want to welcome the wondrous new breeds of animals who are soon coming to inhabit this beautiful planet in the radiance of the New Earth. But this time, Angelo says, they will not come until the violence has stopped and they are assured of being welcomed as Brothers.

Chapter One

A Message From Angelo to All People on this Planet

Angelo, the Angel Cat, speaks on Behalf of all Beings of the Animal Kingdom on this Planet.

Introduction by Angelo

MY NAME IS ANGELO. I was born May 31, 1994. I have returned to Earth once again with my good friend, Tender-Heart. I would like to remain humble, but I have to admit that I am quite a handsome blue-point Balinese cat, and Tender-Heart is a beautiful white, long-haired cat. We are both Angel Cats and we come from the angelic realm of cats in God's Animal Kingdom. Our planet is just one of several cat planets. My friend, Tender-Heart, is a healing cat. On my planet Khaath, I am one of the rulers, and I am known also as a spiritual teacher. When I am not incarnated on Earth, I am what you would consider the equivalent of a prince. I am considered royalty. We are both neutered males of the same age, and we have both been cats a long, long time in many cat bodies on Earth. We are very good friends and because of our long-lasting friendship we spend much time together between lives. As a matter of fact, we have been cats on Earth, in and out of incarnation, for centuries. When we met again in this life, we recognized each other instantly, and it was a touching moment for me to see my old friend again.

Angelo (far right)

I was born from my mother, Saffire, along with my four other siblings in Aurelia Louise's house. Three of my siblings found nice, loving homes and don't live with us anymore; but my sister Precious, who went to another home for one year, came back to live with us again after a bad experience. When we were small, I was the biggest kitten of the litter. That is how my "mom," Aurelia Louise, could tell me apart from the others, because Balinese cats are born totally white and take about six weeks to show their markings.

Several months later, when Aurelia Louise found Tender-Heart and brought him home, I was thrilled to see my old buddy again. Tender-Heart knew that he came to Earth to be with Aurelia Louise again in this life, and also to be with me. He was born about one mile from our house, one month before me. When he was one year old, since Aurelia Louise had not shown up in his life, he decided to leave his home to find her. He was not sure exactly where she lived when he ventured away from his house.

Tender-Heart

In the process of looking for her, he got lost. He became sick, very hungry, weak and quite skinny. He was a few weeks on the road in his pursuit to find Aurelia Louise, and he nearly died. One day, in April 1995, Aurelia Louise was taking a walk in a field near a highway a couple miles from our house and he saw her. He was almost too weak to walk to her, but he knew this could be his only chance. He struggled to make his way to her as his little heart was leaping with joy in hopes that she would recognize him and take him home. When he came close and she saw him, she started talking to him with gentleness. Tender-Heart said to me: "I put my two front paws on her knees and looked at her directly in the eyes. I tried to convey to her telepathically, as well as I could with my cat body, that I wanted her to take me home. She did not recognize me at first, but she received part of my message and took me home anyway. She felt sorry for me because I was so sick, hungry and weak. As soon as she took me in her arms, I relaxed and stretched my body close to hers to let her know that I was grateful, and that she was my person, the one I had been looking for."

"When I arrived at her house, I was so hopeful! I knew then that I was in the right place, and that she would nurse me back to health; and she did. When I saw you, Angelo, I recognized you right away. I wanted to jump on you and play, but I was too weak. I was so happy when you came close to welcome me and stayed near me during the months of my recovery."

In our past lives, we both had some good lives and some sad ones as cats. This life is very pleasant for us. We are enjoying a wonderful home with Aurelia Louise. We get lots of love and many kisses each day, a warm place to lay our bodies and good healthy food. We also get to share her bed at night when we want to. She talks to us a lot and we have a profound bonding. This makes us very mellow cats as we feel loved and understood. We can go on doing what we have come to do in this life, and we are helping her with her work in our own way.

Animals' Purposes

Animals' purposes on this Earth are neither obvious to humans nor well understood. I wish to convey to humans the important message that all animals come to Earth with a special purpose from the Creator and from the Earth Mother, which they intend to fulfill when they are not interrupted and prevented by humans. Aurelia Louise understands this and provides the proper environment in which we can easily fulfill our work and missions here in our cat bodies. We help with the grids of the Earth and our work, in a sense, is more etheric than purely physical.

Cats are meditators and help balance the energies of the planet. Their energies are more closely related to Feminine Energy. It is most important for all cats to be allowed to touch the Earth and be free to do so whenever we feel the need. This is part of our work. So many cats are never given the chance to touch the Earth. We work closely with the Earth Mother who is our Goddess. We are also greeters, healers and companions for people. We sing our song of love to you with our purring. Our purring is calming and soothing to humans. We come into incarnation to help a specific person, but often we are abandoned and rejected by the very person we have come here to help. Cats often take into their bodies negative emotions and energies from their person and their surroundings. This helps their caretaker tremendously, as it "lightens their load." It often prevents many health problems for them. We consider ourselves "buffers" for mankind.

Dogs' purposes are different. Their energies are more closely related to Male Energy. They are faithful companions and protectors for humans. They have very powerful spirits. They possess an ability and willingness to love, even when abused; and their example is one of the most important lessons humans need to learn in order to fulfill their divine destiny. Dogs are great teachers of unconditional love for their human companions. They also take human emotions into their bodies; they suffer in silence and without complaining. They love unconditionally and endlessly. Even when they are poorly treated, they are still willing to love. It takes a tremendous amount of abuse and neglect for a dog to stop loving. In fulfilling their purpose, dogs help humans in a more physical way than cats do. They also have their own dog heaven on their own planet where they go to rest between their earthly lives.

In a nutshell, cats' purposes are more subtle and spiritual, and dogs' purposes are more physical and down to earth. Neither one is better than the other; they are simply complementary and both benefit humans. In general, humans don't know about this, and far too many continue to treat animals as if they have no purpose and no feelings. Many humans refuse to recognize that all animals are various manifestations and extensions of God, and all are as precious to God as any other Creation. God loves all of His vast Creation and considers all living creatures with utmost respect and sacredness. In God's Eyes none are lower or better than any others; they are all "perfect" the way they are. Because of the great diversity in Creation, animals are just "different" from humans. God expects humans to extend the same love and compassion toward all living beings as they wish to receive for themselves.

Every animal on this planet is here to fulfill a purpose or assignment given by the Great Creator. When humans kill them without their permission, their purpose remains unfulfilled and the planet and its inhabitants suffer more for it. We truly are your younger brothers and sisters on the ladder of evolution.

We look up to humans to receive help, love and compassion the same way you look to angels to receive help, love and compassion. As you receive from the higher realms, you must pass the same onto others of younger evolution. No one can ever kill any of us or inflict pain in any form without creating for themselves a situation that will sooner or later manifest as pain or violence in their own lives. This is a Universal Law.

Animal Kingdoms

The Cat kingdom is ruled and guided by wonderful, loving, intelligent, great cat beings called the "Feline Species Elemental Guardians" and "Feline Species Guardian Angels." They are magnificent, loving, gentle and caring Beings of impressive stature. In the spirit world, there are many cat planets, and I come from one of them, called Khaath, a sixth-dimensional planet situated in the galaxy of the God Star, Sirius.

We are much more intelligent than you give us credit for; and when we do not have the limitations of our physical bodies on Earth, our intelligence is the quality and magnitude of the sixth-dimensional consciousness. We consider ourselves as intelligent as any human, and very often, more so. In fact, we can communicate telepathically, while most humans have lost this ability. We have an extended vision enabling us to see beyond the physical dimension, an ability also lost by the human kingdom. We thrive on a simple existence, and we cannot understand why humans are so intent on complicating their lives the way they do. In reality, life on Earth could be very simple and wondrous.

The Dog Kingdom is ruled and guided by equally wonderful, great dog Spirit Beings called the "Canine Species Elemental Guardians" and "Canine Species Guardian Angels." They come from many dog planets and are wonderful, magnificent beings of impressive stature. As well, horses have their own guides called "Equine Species Elemental Guardians" and "Equine Species Guardian Angels," and they also have their own equine home planets which are mostly sixth-dimensional consciousness. All animal kingdoms in the vastness of Creation have their own planets and hierarchy. The vastness of the animal kingdoms is of such magnitude that it is beyond most humans' ability to understand.

Each animal species has its own guides and rulers who care for them, and are in charge of the heavenly realm for that species. All animals in their heavenly kingdoms are much more beautiful than the ones you see on Earth, and we consider our earthly bodies only temporary, just like you do. You are also magnificent in your spiritual body.

Aurelia Louise is very conscious of animal guardian angels and uses their services quite often when she is aware of an animal in need of special help. She likes using them because she gets very good results when calling upon them for help. Most humans on Earth do not know about animal guardian angels and never call them. When someone calls upon them, they are happy to be of assistance and rush to help immediately. Aurelia Louise calls the Feline Guardians when there is a problem with a cat, and she is always amazed with the results.

Aurelia Louise told me that when my mother, Saffire, was a kitten, she used to roam a lot and became lost frequently. Every time Aurelia Louise lost her, she would call to the Feline Species Elemental Guardians for help in finding her. She said that each time, somehow, as if by magic, a little while later Saffire would find her way back home or someone would bring her back. Finally she asked the Feline Species Elemental Guardians to put some cat angels around the fence in the yard to stop Saffire from getting out. Aurelia Louise said that from then on for almost a year, she never left the yard and never got lost.

When my mother, Saffire, was ready for mating, Aurelia Louise wanted a beautiful, similar breed male cat who looked like her. She was unable to locate one, so she made a request to the Feline Species Elemental Guardians to send an appropriate male cat for Saffire. Guess what? A few hours later...there he was...an extremely handsome, well-mannered, friendly Himalayan cat showed up at the door. They mated, and sixty-four days later, two beautiful kittens, half Balinese and half Himalayan, were born.

At the time the kittens were born, Saffire was still very young, not even a year old. She did not understand what was happening to her and did not know what to do. When the kittens were born, she was afraid and made no attempt to care for them. She tried to pull away from them. Aurelia Louise was watching and trying to help, but she became worried that the new-born kittens would suffer or die if their mother did not take care of them soon enough. Aurelia Louise tried to show Saffire what to do with no success. She then remembered the Feline Species Elemental Guardians and called to them for help. They came immediately. Aurelia Louise then related the problem to them and asked them to explain to Saffire, in their familiar cat language, what was happening and to show her how to care for her babies.

Within a few minutes, Saffire started to lick and care for her newborn babies and never stopped licking them for weeks thereafter. She proved herself to be a most wonderful and devoted cat mother. I was watching this from my place in Cat Heaven. I wanted to come back on Earth again as a cat to be with Aurelia Louise once more, and I knew that Saffire would be my mother the next time.

A year later, about the same time, Saffire gave birth to her second litter. This is when I was born, along with my siblings. Aurelia Louise called the Feline Species Elemental Guardians for help prior to the birth. She asked them to oversee the delivery and make sure everything would go smoothly. They came to assist our birth in their spiritual cat bodies, and the birth unfolded as perfectly as expected. Saffire knew exactly what to do this time.

Saffire, Angelo and siblings

She gave us wonderful loving care. Aurelia Louise watched carefully but did not have to intervene like she did the first time.

The Feline Guardians play the same role for cats as guardian angels do for humans. They are not usually visible to the human eye, but on occasion some people see them.

I will describe for you what they may look like. Their appearance may vary a little, but in general they are quite big, the size of a lion or bigger, but looking very much like a domestic cat. They are much more beautiful than any domestic cat ever seen on Earth. The one Aurelia Louise saw had very beautiful, shiny, silky, white, long hair with big, kind green eyes.

These highly evolved Cat Beings are so loving and gentle, no one would ever be afraid of them. They represent dedication and unconditional love for the cat kingdom and all Life.

Angelo (far right) and siblings

Chapter Two

Important Message From Angelo and Tender-Heart

Angelo speaks

OUR MESSAGE IS NOT ONLY CONCERNING CATS, but all animals of "God's Kingdom." You see, many people do not yet realize that animals are not born as inanimate objects, to be used and misused for profit and experimentation. Domestic animals are sent to Earth to become companions to the special person assigned to them. So often they are abused and abandoned by the very person they have come to love and help.

Dogs were never meant to be left outside, chained by themselves in the cold, wet, or heat, day in and day out. Their spirits have the quality of being very loving, faithful friends and companions. They need to be living and bonded with the people who have taken responsibility for adopting them. Dogs become mean and troublesome only when they have been improperly bred or handled. Humans have created many new breeds of dogs by using genetic manipulations. Many of these breeds do not fulfill God's original intent and should not be acquired. It will be a blessing when certain breeds become extinct or leave the planet because they do not belong here.

Too many dogs lead lonely and unhappy lives. They are pack animals, and are meant to be living with others. Dogs, by nature, are not loners. It makes us very sad to see so many dogs wrongly treated. Excuse us if we repeat ourselves, we just want to make sure you understand.

We, of the animal kingdom, have gifts to bring to Earth and to humans. We are also here to fulfill God's purposes, just as you are. Too many times our gifts cannot be offered and our purpose remains unfulfilled because of the ways we are treated. Many of us are killed before we ever get a chance to offer anything at all.

The main difference between animals and humans is that we retain the ability to remember our divinity while so many of you have forgotten. Our purposes are different from yours, however, they are complementary, and considered by us, of the animal kingdom, just as important. Simply because we do not speak the human language does not mean we do not think and have no feelings. We are much more intelligent than humans give us credit for and we experience the same quality of feelings. We can experience cold, hunger, pain, sadness, abandonment, loneliness, fear, joy, etc. with the same intensity humans do.

Our fate is often painful because humans have lost the ability to communicate with us telepathically, and so our needs often go unrecognized. When humans used to communicate with us, they understood our level of intelligence. They had great love and respect for all of us. It was mutual and there were no aggressive animals on Earth like there are today.

Farm Animals

From the beautiful and peaceful heavenly realms of the animal kingdoms, we are able to observe much of what is happening to animals on this planet. Animal exploitation on Earth, especially farm animals, has become the ultimate human abomination.

**Out of the millions of planets that are inhabited by various civilizations, most of them host many species of animals.
Did you know that nowhere else in all the Universes, among the thousands of galaxies and millions of stars and planets, are animals as badly treated as they are here on Earth? This abomination qualifies humans on this planet to be considered "primitive" and "undeveloped" by other civilizations of the Universe.**

The animal kingdom's purposes have been terribly misunderstood here. Millions upon millions of animals every year are severely abused, caged, starved, abandoned, hunted, killed, and slaughtered all over the planet. Many millions more are tortured by your scientists for useless experiments. But we keep returning to Earth again and again, hoping that someday humans' hearts will soften with a new understanding that we are here to play an important role in your evolutionary process. God has designed life on Earth in such a way that humans and animals need each other.

Could you imagine a world without animals and animals without humans? We all need each other, but mutual respect has to be accorded in order for this planet and its people to experience, once again, brotherhood, love, peace, and the abundant life for all.

Nearly all farm animals are now treated and raised strictly to maximize profit for their owners. There is rarely any consideration given to the intentions, feelings or comfort of these animals.

Humans are still as cruel to farm animals as ever before. Although animal farming has taken a different form in the last decades, it is certainly no better than it used to be. As a matter of fact, it becomes more cruel as the years go by.

Farm animals are often treated like products. All their rights and feelings are totally denied.

A very long time ago when I was a horse in a previous experience, I remember I was not very well treated; I hated the experience of being a horse. I decided to never again return to Earth as a horse. I much prefer being a cat, and I have been a cat for a long time. Most farm animals' natural lifestyle and social needs are totally denied. They represent dollars to their so-called "owners."

If you knew how chickens and eggs are commercially produced, and the level of misery chickens are subjected to for their entire lives, you would think twice about eating them. This applies to almost all meat commercially produced.

The flesh you eat when buying commercially produced meats is the product of pain and suffering. It may be acceptable to eat some animal flesh from time to time, but there is a right and a wrong way of doing it.

• You should always give thanks for the animal who has sacrificed its life for your nourishment, and bless the animal. Stop a moment to offer your gratitude.

• Eat only the flesh of animals who have been raised in a loving way and who are killed with dignity.

- When you ingest meat into your body from animals who have suffered much abuse, you are taking this into your body, which can result in problems with your health because you have absorbed this negative vibration.

- Buy your eggs, chicken and other meats only from free-range farming. If you move to the country, when possible, raise your own meat and eggs in a natural environment.

Farm animals in the last few decades have received the worst treatment ever inflicted by humans.

The modern ways of raising farm animals for food have become one of the worst tragedies and crimes committed against the animal kingdom. Soon to come in the not so distant future is a great cosmic accountability for all those who have mistreated animals. It is not my purpose to scare you. Only know that history always repeats itself when people do not learn their lessons of love and compassion. It will soon repeat itself again for those who are accountable.

I, Angelo, want to tell you about many lessons you will not want to hear. It is easier for you to learn about them now than suffer the consequences.

They are the unlearned lessons that are responsible for the pains, sorrows, distress and sagas of the human race.

Please listen to my message.

"Whatever abuse or violence is inflicted on animals, sooner or later, (this lifetime or the next), will eventually be transferred and experienced by humans. This is an inescapable Divine Law. Please be aware of the suffering of farm animals, and how so many of them are raised in merciless ways, ending their lives in cruel methods of slaughter. You must know that what you are ingesting into your bodies when you eat dead animal flesh is, most of the time, the product of abuse and immense suffering. Many humans are creating for themselves a painful and sick future through the treatment of farm and other animals. It is happening all around you.

"The book, *Diet for A New America*, explains all this very well, our 'mom,' Aurelia Louise told us. We recommend that you read this as well as the book, *Animal Liberation*. It will help you develop a more compassionate heart for animals and their suffering at the hands of unconscious humans.

"Whether you inflict pain on another human or on an animal, the accountability is the same. Like it or not, deny it or not, the great law applies. Any pain you create for any other form of life, no matter what it is, is a pain that you are creating for yourself.

"Did you ever wonder why so many people are sick and suffering all kinds of ailments, pains, diseases, violence and various problems on this planet?"

We Have Equal Rights To Share Planet Earth Without Being Abused

The time has come for humans to accept that this planet is hosting the human kingdom and the animal kingdom equally. Humans think they have all the power over us, and that we have no rights because we do not speak the same language or because we are different. If humans would tune into the **Love frequency,** they would realize that we, of the animal kingdom, are just as precious and important to God as any of His other Creations. We are all playing different roles in the Divine Grand Master Plan.

We were meant to cohabit this planet with humans in a loving and peaceful manner. God's intent is for all of us to help each other without abuse or violence. We are meant to teach each other the true meaning of Love and Compassion. Animals are not inferior or superior to humans; we are different. The language of the Universe is the language of Love. One does not need to speak with "words" to know and speak this language.

**When God gave humans
"Dominion over the Earth,"
it was not meant as permission to abuse animals.**

On the contrary, it is a unique opportunity for humans to learn the lessons of love, kindness, understanding and compassion toward each other, toward animals, and all other forms of life. No human can ever hope to enter into the Kingdom of God without learning these lessons. We are all helpers and teachers for each other.

In the beginning, in the far distant past of Earth history, humans and animals cohabited lovingly and peacefully. They communicated with each other telepathically, and they were so in tune and in harmony with each other, that communication in the human language was not necessary. We understood and loved each other, and we helped each other in very practical ways. There was no violence. There was no fear nor mistrust between us. It was a time of abundance, prosperity, peace, and love for all. Only true love and compassion for all can bring back permanent prosperity to the human race.

Humans then had no need to show superiority by requesting submission from animals. Mutual respect was the order of the day. This was an ancient time when the lamb laid down beside the lion and the little child led them.

In the present time, this concept is almost forgotten by the people of Earth. When people lived their lives with compassion for animals in their hearts, we were loved and appreciated as legitimate and rightful neighbors on this planet. Now, human hearts have hardened toward us.

And we, the Beings of the Animal Kingdom,
have been reduced by humans
to mere commodities to
be traded for profit.

How painful this betrayal is for us! This abuse by so many humans has driven away our former trust and love. For good reason animals, in general, now fear humans. Thank goodness there are still many humans who love and respect animals. Aurelia Louise tells us that she loves us so much, that we are like her special children, and that her commitment to us is for life...until death separates us.

On our planet, when we study the records of human behavior, we can see that past history has shown again and again that the bad treatment inflicted on animals sooner or later is transferred to the human race. That is why Tender-Heart and I so urgently want humans to understand the importance of our message. You only have to look into the terrors of the past, current politics and wars to see what humans have, and still are, inflicting upon other humans.

Will you please hear our message with your hearts, my friends?

As long as humans are cruel to animals, they will be cruel to each other. When humans learn to be kind to animals, they will be kind to each other.

"O people of the Earth Mother, hear us, Angelo and Tender-Heart, the angel cats. Our message is most important for your future happiness. By cosmic law, by the great laws that govern this Universe, it will not be possible for God to allow the human race to enjoy the long-awaited golden age as long as human hearts are hardened. It simply cannot happen until all of Life is treated with love, dignity and sacredness."

This love applies to the human kingdom, the animal kingdom, the elemental kingdom and the plant kingdom alike. We need to express a deep respect and gratitude for our Beloved Mother Earth who is willingly and lovingly hosting our evolution. We, of the animal kingdom, when incarnated on Earth, have a very close and personal relationship with the Earth Mother. We are the offspring of one of Her many kingdoms. She loves and considers each one of us as one of Her many children. She loves each human the same way. She considers each one of you as one of Her many children also.

But you ignore Her love and Her endless patience with humanity. You destroy and pollute Her body without any thought. She is distressed by the fact that humans act as if they have a right to "own" the animal kingdom and dispose of us as you please.

Please become more aware that the Earth Mother is hosting us, as she is hosting you. Humans cannot morally own each other, nor can they morally own animals; humans are simply caretakers of the animals. We belong to the Earth Mother in our hearts, and we assist Her in many ways that you are not aware of.

You have forgotten that you are only a guest here, just like us. None of you can own the Earth, nor any of its many kingdoms. You only think you do. If you think you can, I say it is an illusion. You cannot take any of it with you when you leave the planet. You live here only a few short years. The Earth Mother is here forever.

The Earth Mother is Sovereign.

Cats, dogs and horses are still very forgiving, but millions of wild animals no longer want to have anything to do with humans; some species are violent with them when given the chance. To this day, millions of domestic animals are subjected to a life of loneliness, abandonment, pain, betrayal, sickness and hunger by humans. Not all animals are as lucky as Tender-Heart and I are in having such a loving and caring human companion.

Because of the abuse of domestic animals, many choose to incarnate as wild animals, in spite of the challenges that animals in the wild have to endure.

My mother, Saffire, a beautiful Balinese cat, was a raccoon in her last life. She was quite afraid to be subjected to the domestication of humans. While still in the feline heaven, she was promised by the Feline Species Elemental Guardians that if she agreed to come to Earth to experience life as a domestic cat, they would see to it that she would be in the care of a kind person. When she checked Aurelia Louise's past records, she saw that Aurelia Louise had always been compassionate with animals. She accepted the challenge, and we live happily together in a loving home.

My mother Saffire

"Any religion which is not based on a respect for life is not a true religion.
*Until he extends his circle of compassion **to all living things**, man himself will not find peace."*

–Albert Schweitzer

Chapter Three

Animals Are Not "Disposable" We all have souls!

Angelo

OUR SOULS ARE PART OF A GROUP CONSCIOUSNESS as are yours. This means that there is less difference between humans and animals on the ladder of evolution than between humans and the masters, angels and beings of the higher realms, whose help you constantly seek.

As you look up to them for help, love, mercy and compassion, we look up to you for the same assistance. As you receive from those above you on the ladder of evolution, it is necessary that you extend the same love and compassion to your brothers and sisters, just a step behind. This is a cosmic obligation. All Creation is an endless chain of manifestation from the Creator, from the smallest to the greatest. Truly, We Are All One! As one part of Creation is hurting and suffering, the Whole is also affected. It cannot be otherwise.

Hear us:

We are not disposable possessions.
We are like family members.
Too many people acquire pets
without the thought of a
long-term commitment.

We are "lifetime companions" and feel very betrayed and heartbroken when you abandon, reject and dispose of us as mere commodities.

Because we are so cute and cuddly when we are babies, we are very popular. When pets are no longer the irresistible little puppies or adorable kittens, millions of pets are abandoned on roads, city parks or shelters. This is no love at all. They end up having to fend for themselves and suffer cold, betrayal, rejection, and hunger until, occasionally, a kind person picks them up to take care of them or until they die a painful death.

Millions of humans do not give
a second thought to the frightful
fate of abandoned animals.

For those who die in this manner, it is a very painful death. However, it is not as painful as those animals in research laboratories who suffer and are subjected to the most cruel treatment ever created by humans. They are caged and tortured until they die of pain and sorrow or until they are ruthlessly killed.

When God and the angels see and feel the plight and hear the lamentations of those dear little ones, they shed big tears.

Animal Experiments in Research Labs

The Great Creator is very concerned with the cruelty and heartlessness that those so-called "scientists" in white coats do to His Little Ones of the Animal Kingdom.

They perform their cruelties in private research labs, universities, hospitals and government agencies around the world. All this in the name of "science." Can you believe that? How primitive and arrogant can these scientists be? They refuse to understand that there is never any need to test anything on animals at the cost of so much suffering.

There are so many other humane alternatives that are much more effective. Why are they not using them? It is all a question of money and greed, not research for real answers. All answers are contained within oneself.

There is never a need to put any other form of life through endless pain and torture. Animal experiments are the product of indifference toward animal life by those who arrogantly assume the right to submit animals to pain and suffering for their own selfish ends. What these researchers do to the animals they experiment with is more barbaric than any of past caveman behavior. The cavemen in primitive time had more compassion for us than your present-day scientists do.

Using animals for human experiments is totally unacceptable in the eyes of our Creator. In a world where people consider themselves "enlightened" or "civilized," this behavior is shameful! Animal experimentation, in the name of science, is degrading for the human race. It is the equivalent of the practice of voodoo and black magic.

New methods of testing products exist that are so much more accurate, humane and economical. When people are in tune with Divine laws, they know what to do for their welfare. They do not need to force painful experiments on animals to find out.

Animal experimentation keeps torturing millions of animals year after year. In the majority of cases, they are not seeking scientific data or even trying to learn anything new from these experiments. They have repeated the same experiments year after year just to keep their "grant money" active and secure.

Perhaps as much as ninety percent (90%) of this abominable research is supported with your tax dollars.

Your tax funds flow into their pockets and their phony results are their job protection. Often the results are manipulated to fulfill the desired outcome at the expense of innocent animals. Animal experimentation shows a total disregard for the purpose of the animals on Earth. Please read the books *Animal Liberation* and *Stolen for Profit.* You will learn much more. Perhaps it will make your hair curl or it will open your heart when you read about the atrocities animals still have to endure in your society, financed and sanctioned by your government authorities.

Nothing very positive could ever come out of torturing innocent and defenseless animals.

Animal research and experimentation are an assault on the Animal Kingdom. The results cannot be trusted as these experiments are conducted without love and under abnormal circumstances.

In the U.S. alone, an average of 80 million animals are being bred and sacrificed for this despicable purpose each year.

In order for mankind to evolve into a golden age of enlightenment, this animal abuse has to stop! Humans will not find proper solutions to human problems as long as they are cruel and insensitive to other forms of life, including the animals.

**Will you help?
Know that Heaven is Weeping
for Us on Earth!**

We are sorry to repeat ourselves so many times but we are trying to get the point across. We don't know how to speak to humans in order to touch their hearts and make them understand.

**Perhaps you can do something about
improving the treatment of animals
on this planet. There are always
big and small ways everyone can help.**

Abandoned Animals

It is true that many more people have pets and give them wonderful homes like my buddy, Tender-Heart, and I have this time around. However, God weeps over the over 50,000,000 domestic cats and dogs abandoned by their owners each year in the U.S.A., and many more millions around the rest of the world. Most of them never know human love and tenderness again. These animals never have the opportunity to fulfill the purposes for which they have come to Earth.

This human wickedness has to stop! Humans have developed a very "disposable" society, and they trash everything they no longer want or need, including their pets, their unborn children, etc. You know what

I mean...I hope. Yes, I repeat myself, approximately 50,000,000 of us are betrayed and abandoned by our owners each year.

Do you know that out of this number, about 20,000,000 animals are abandoned on public roads, in the forest, or parks, or wherever it is convenient to drop them off.

**Are you aware of the pain and
the suffering and the fate
of the abandoned animals?**

Most of them die of hunger, cold, starvation, loneliness and a broken heart. Many of them are beaten and chased away when they beg for a morsel of food, and they become afraid of humans.

Out of those 20,000,000, a small percentage, perhaps 5 to 8%, are found by kind people and given a loving home again. The fate of the others makes God and the angels cringe. They die a painful death. They are received on the "other side" by the legions of angels who are assigned to the endless task of healing animals of the traumas acquired by their life experience among humans on Earth.

In other instances, pets are taken to animal shelters where the animal owners naively believe that their pet will be given to a nice home.

What the people in the shelters don't tell them is that many shelters (usually in the larger cities) sell those innocent little animals to research labs for a fate worse than death. Again, animals are traded off for profit.

People who cannot make a life-time commitment to their pets should not adopt pets in the first place. They are not responsible enough, or simply not in a position to adopt a pet for long term companionship.

The Great Master Jesus said:

"And whosoever shall offend one of these little ones that believe in me, it is better for him that a millstone were hanged about his neck, and he were cast into the sea." (Mark 9:42)

When the Great Master made this statement, He was not referring only to human children. He was referring to all sentient beings on this planet, including animals.

We, of the animal kingdom, in our souls, also know Him and revere Him. As a matter of fact, I am going to go as far as telling you that the vast majority of animals, at the level of their souls, know Him and revere Him with more sincerity than most humans do. If you are surprised and have a tendency to think that animals do not know their Creator, if you think that animals do not know anything or cannot feel as much as humans in their soul...think again and meditate on it. You may realize that you are in serious need of a new education concerning animals.

Do you know that all your actions, both good and bad, are recorded in your "Book of Life," and you are held accountable? You will have to live with the consequences of those actions until every negative action is fully amended by Pure Love. This law applies to all beings in all Universes. Humans on Planet Earth are not exempt. This is an immutable Cosmic Law.

Just a Cat?

You may not be inclined to take my message too seriously because you may say that I am "Just a Cat." Yes, in my present form, according to most human thinking, I am just a cat. But I have been around for a very long time, and throughout the centuries and the millennia, I have learned a lot.

I am a cat with a past, with knowledge and with perception. In my spiritual body, I am much more than a cat.

If you would have me as one of your earthly teachers, I can take you a long way in your return journey to "paradise." Tender-Heart is a healing cat, and he knows much about healing. He can teach you many things.

Every day my buddies and I lie together in our basket and we do a lot of meditating. We try to think of ways we can touch human hearts regarding the improvement of treatment of animals on this planet.

Tender-Heart

I have another buddy I want to mention. His name is Sunny. He is a short-haired, orange cat. He came to live at our house when he was no longer wanted by his former caretakers. At least they did not abandon him on a deserted country road. They brought him to our house, and they asked Aurelia Louise to find him a new home. That never happened and he has continued to live with us.

Sunny

He is very quiet and doesn't say much, but he is a profound thinker! He is new at being a cat. It is only his second lifetime as a cat. Sunny was abused when he was small, and he is still afraid of people he does not know. I have a feeling that someday he will also give his message and reveal the pain he is bearing in his heart.

He likes living with us because he feels secure here since he doesn't fully trust people yet. In his last life, he told me he was abused and totally neglected. He died a painful death, alone, sick and hungry, trapped in a brick wall when he was less than a year old.

In this life, he trusts only Aurelia Louise and her friends who love cats. He told me that he is still afraid of being sent to another home. He is quiet and docile. He hopes that if he causes no problems and makes no demands, he will win the privilege of staying here the rest of his life. He is obedient and shows Aurelia Louise a lot of gratitude. I know that Aurelia Louise loves him too and thinks he is very sweet.

We kind of consider him as a younger brother even though he is almost the same age we are, because he is so new at being a cat and so often insecure. We pretend to protect him and he is learning from us.

Angelo

Chapter Four

Young Animals and Children

HA! I ALMOST FORGOT... I want to tell you more about my sister, Precious.

Precious

When Precious was still quite small, a woman and three children came to our house and wanted to take her home with them. Aurelia Louise was hesitant to let her go at first because she was so beautiful and gentle. The children really wanted Precious to go with them. She finally agreed, on the condition that they would be kind and gentle with her and promise that, if they ever decided they couldn't keep her, she would be returned to Aurelia Louise.

I did not see Precious again for many seasons; when she came back to our house, she was very sick, skinny and did not want to be touched by anyone. She stayed under a sofa all day where no one could reach her, and she did not want to play anymore. Her pupils were constantly dilated, her back was crooked, and she was suffering with such pounding headaches daily that she wanted out of her body. She was so sick, she almost died. She hissed at Tender-Heart and me. Tender-Heart is such a gentle healing cat that sick cats usually like to go to him for help. He tried many times to come close and befriend her, but she hissed at him every time in fear.

We could see that her back problem was causing the pain in her head, and we knew she was in deep trouble. We tried to tell Aurelia Louise, hoping she would help her. After a few days she got our message and started to examine Precious. She phoned a person who communicated telepathically with all of us.

Precious told this person about her pounding headaches and the severe damage at the base of her neck that was causing her so much discomfort. She was very afraid of being touched because each movement caused her more pain.

She also explained that in her former house, with the children, she suffered mishandling. She said that the children loved her very much, but they played with her as if she were a stuffed toy. She said that they used to throw her in the air to see if she would land on her paws. Most of the time she did, but at times she was too sick and she had too much pain to try. Precious said that several times she landed on her neck and back and the pain was atrocious. The children, who did not realize that she was in pain, continued their "game" and she got progressively worse.

As time went on, she quit eating and became very skinny. Every time she tried to eat she would throw up her food. Finally, she became so afraid of everyone she started to hide all the time. Because she was not so playful anymore and hissed at the children, the people brought her back to our house.

They thought Precious had become mean. They did not realize the children were the cause of her problems.

Precious is very loving and gentle when handled properly.

Aurelia Louise was furious when she found out what these people had done to her little Precious. She took Precious to a doctor several times who works on backs and necks, and Aurelia Louise did special treatments on her a couple times a day along with a massage. She also gave Precious special remedies several times a day to help her feel better. Aurelia Louise did this every day for several months. She gave Precious a lot of extra love and attention, and promised her that if she recovered, Aurelia Louise would keep her safe with us for the rest of her life. Precious liked being in this house and she cooperated.

Very, very slowly, with all this tender loving care, Precious started getting better and was not so afraid anymore. She gradually became friendlier and no longer hid under the sofa. Her pupils returned to normal little by little, and she stopped avoiding us.

After four months, she played with Sunny for the first time. She has become very attached to Aurelia Louise. She follows her everywhere. After six months, her back was no longer hurting her, the pain in her neck was much better, and her headaches were almost gone. She only had them once in a while and they were not so severe. She could eat her food without throwing up and she gained all her weight back. She is now again beautiful, loving and friendly. We are very honored to have her as part of our family team. She is still very quiet and keeps somewhat to herself, but I think that with a little more time she will be 100% recovered.

I heard Aurelia Louise phone the people who had Precious for that one year and tell them about the situation. She explained how much pain Precious was suffering because of their improper handling. I remember her telling the parents that children and teenagers need constant supervision when handling young animals. She also explained they needed to teach their children the proper way to treat animals, or they should not have pets.

Precious said to me that the children were not malicious but did not understand just how much pain they were causing her. To them, she was a beautiful living toy.

Precious with Angelo

The message from Angelo, the Angel cat, is that young cats and puppies should not be given to children as toys. They are too delicate. If you want your children to have pets, and I think that it is good for children to have pets, please give them "older" animals to play with. They are not so vulnerable to improper treatment, as they can defend themselves better by running away when mistreated.

I know that children rarely mistreat animals on purpose. They do so from lack of awareness of what hurts the animal, and they sometimes mistakenly use them as toys. It is not their fault; nevertheless, children should be closely supervised and taught properly.

Aurelia Louise told me that she went to see the family

to explain further. The parents and children felt very badly when they heard how much pain they had caused Precious, but could then better understand her behavior. It made the children cry, and they all promised to never do this again to a cat or any animal. My sweet sister, Precious, was the victim of unsupervised children and suffered much because of it.

There are many millions of
pets who suffer a similar fate
in the hands of children, who rarely
figure out why their loving pets are
not so loving anymore.

I know that Aurelia Louise would never give me away. I am very secure with her. She told me that if anything ever happened to her, and if she would have to leave this world before we do, that she would make special financial arrangements for all of us to stay together somewhere in a loving place as long as we live. I call this Responsible Stewardship of Animal Life.

Pet Shops

Pet shops sell good things for pets, but when you buy your animal companion in a pet store, most often they come from puppy and kitty mills. It is a poor policy to encourage these greedy breeders. They are not breeding animals out of love. They see them strictly as "objects of profit" and don't care what happens to the animal later on. They also are not concerned about creating a surplus population of pets who then end up being euthanized in shelters. Their only concern seems to be how much money they can make.

Since we live between 10 and 20 years, providing good homes for all of us cannot keep up with such careless and excessive breeding programs that are just for profit. This creates a severe imbalance, a great overabundance of pet population. Please don't buy your pets from pet shops. You are encouraging a harmful business when you do. Many puppy and kitty mills aim to produce an average of 3,000 to 4,000 puppies and kittens a month. This is how 50,000,000 of them end up abandoned and euthanized each year. This is a severe misuse of creative energy.

Instead, seriously consider adopting abandoned animals and give a pet, who is hurting from a broken heart, a loving home again. Most of them will make loving and loyal pets.

My "mom," Aurelia Louise, adopts only abandoned animals, and has always been blessed with all of us. She said she would never pay money for any animal because no animal should be considered "a saleable item." They belong to the Earth Mother, not to humans. To have one in your care is nothing but a privilege.

Humans can only be caretakers and friends of animals. As far as Aurelia Louise is concerned, it is immoral to be in the animal market for profit.

"If you can't be in the animal business out of pure Love for them and for their welfare, please leave them to those humans who can honor them for who they really are.
Please don't ever use them for profit."

Aurelia Louise says she is happy to give money to help with the operating costs of animal shelters which do not sell their animals for research, and whose focus is to find loving homes for those who have been abandoned or lost. It costs money to operate shelters, and the work is a labor of Love. Often their management is done by volunteers. Most shelters are overpopulated and under-funded.

The gift of an animal is not always obvious to humans, but it is always there. It is a unique privilege to be the caretaker of an animal.

Please spay/neuter your pets.

There are too many of us already on this planet.

Every dog, cat or any other of God's creatures deserves to be loved and cared for in a loving home. Adopting a pet requires loyalty and commitment. I say to all of you again:

**"When you adopt a pet, it is a
serious and long term decision,
because we live for many years
and we are not disposable.
Don't ever adopt a pet lightly."**

No pet deserves to be born to be abandoned or to be used for ruthless experiments in animal research labs just to keep someone on the payroll. You are part of the solution or you are part of the problem. Become a champion for the rights and welfare of animals, and I promise you shall be blessed more than you can imagine.

A solution may be to decrease the number of pets born yearly until every one has a loving home, and until animal abuse is eliminated in this country and around the world.

**Animals will teach you the art of
unconditional love; they will give you
the opportunity to develop intuition,
tolerance and a compassionate heart.
They will help you grow as a human.
They may also help with your emotional
and physical burdens to make your life
easier. This is a secret most humans
have not yet discovered.**

Domestic Animals

Cats and dogs are not the only beings of the animal kingdom who suffer at the hands of humans. Horses throughout history have had more than their share of abuse by humans. The history of horse abuse on this planet is so great that it would take many books to tell only a small portion of it. I have much to say about this because I was a horse once in another life, and I feel sorry for many horses. I never want to be a horse again. I much prefer to be a cat. At least it is easier to run away when you are in the hands of an insensitive person.

I know that horses are very courageous in accepting the challenge of coming to this planet. They have been used and misused for eons and not appreciated for their service.

The Slaughter of Horses

Are you aware that every day hundreds, perhaps thousands, of horses are sent to various slaughter houses around this country and around the world to be canned as cat and dog food, or flown to Europe to be eaten by humans as very "special steaks?" These are horses who may be older, sick, not able to perform as well as expected, or just simply because their owners want to trade them for money. They represent nothing more than dollar signs for them; all feelings of compassion and loyalty are put aside. This shows complete disregard for the Great Spirit Beings who inhabit these horse bodies.

Horses are sold on the U.S. market for a dollar a pound of body weight. This represents big money for horse dealers, who purchase horses at auctions only to haul them ruthlessly to slaughter houses. If you ever saw the gross cruelty used in their slaughter and the atrocities they suffer to become steaks or cat and dog food, you would be sick at heart. Probably, you would never be the same again; your heart would open and you would become more compassionate.

Horse dealers do not want to hear that horses are great beings who possess very great spirits and are meant to be helpers and companions to humans. It is only on planet Earth where "primitive" humans have so little consideration for horses and other animals. They are revered everywhere else with much respect and appreciation. They have great intelligence and open hearts. Their normal life span is around 30 to 35 years or more. How many actually live their normal lifespan here on earth?

To all those of you who call yourselves "horse lovers:"

- If you are continuing to breed a surplus of horses on this planet just for the fun of having "cute" little colts in your fields or for show and pride, *you are no horse lover.*

- If you are selling your horse to horse dealers when your horse no longer meets your fancy, *you are no horse lover.*

- If you are really a sincere horse lover, you will keep your horses for their full life span. If this is not your policy, *you are no horse lover.*

You may be fooling yourself but you can never fool the Universe and Its great intelligence.

It would be a greater service to the horse kingdom and a greater act of Love and Mercy to leave them in the spirit world.

Again, humans on this planet are breeding way too many horses each year. They breed them just for the pleasure and sport of it, without any concern for their fate in the next 25 to 35 years of a normal life span. Most breeders are not a bit concerned about what happens to their horses down the road after they are sold. They take no responsibility for their breeding practices. Horses have such a wonderful, beautiful, peaceful home in the spirit world on their sixth-dimensional planet; it is best to leave them there, where they belong, unless you are prepared to give them the consideration they deserve on Earth. They are more loved and happier on their own planet than they are here. Like dogs, horses have a great sense of loyalty to their caretakers, and they are heartbroken when their loyalty is betrayed. Very often, it is the caretakers who need to learn the lessons of loyalty.

Have you ever seen the word "horse meat" on your dog or cat food labels?

The establishment is too embarrassed to write this on labels, and they are allowed to get away with it by those who control labeling regulations. They fear that too many people would be outraged. Ignorance is often considered bliss on this planet. You will instead read on labels "meat" and "meat by-products" with no further explanation.

The spirit of horses has always been a multiple blessing for this planet. The way they have been treated is another source of shame for the human race. Too many horses are disposed of through the cruel use of pulleys and deadly hammers in the slaughter houses.

Angelo declares that it would be a greater blessing if horses left the planet and never came back until mankind becomes more compassionate and enlightened.

Imitate the Native People

Native people still have the sensitivity to see us animals as Brothers. They usually ate animal flesh, yes, but they did it with gratitude and reverence. A minimum of violence and pain was inflicted. They also had the consideration to ask the animal's permission to take its life before killing it for their use. Because many of them were able to communicate telepathically with animals, it was easy for them to ask permission and get a reply. If an animal was not ready to let go of its life, they found one that was. They only killed out of necessity, never for "sport." Killing for sport or for fun is another trait of a primitive and unenlightened society.

When an animal was ready and willing to be taken, it made itself available for an easy and humane killing. It was done in a swift and almost painless manner. Native Indians always thanked the animal for sacrificing its life. Animals are not afraid to die, but they are afraid of painful treatment before they die.

How many farmers, cow and chicken breeders, or horse dealers ask the animals in their care for their permission to be taken to the slaughter houses? How many farmers ask their cow's permission to take its little calf away as soon as it is born? How many farmers consider the natural motherly instinct of their animals, the pain and inner anguish they suffer when their young are taken away before they would be normally weaned?

When she lived in a farming community, Aurelia Louise heard cows cry for days and days out of anguish and a broken heart when their newborn calves were taken away within hours of their birth. The farmers were more interested in the extra money they could make with the milk that the cow produced for her newborn than they were in her happiness and welfare.

In reality, since a cow produces a large amount of milk when she has just delivered a new calf, there is no need for this practice. It might mean a little less milk to sell for the farmer, a little less money, but a much happier cow and calf in the long run, and much less distress for the animals who provide the farmer with his livelihood. Why not make it a win-win situation for all concerned? Aurelia Louise never wanted to have anything to do with these unethical farming practices. She kept her peace and prayed for the angels to come and comfort the distressed animals, but her heart ached for them.

All this unnecessary animal suffering for the sake of profit! How would a farmer and his wife feel if someone came and stole their children each time one was born?

**You may disagree with me,
but I, Angelo,
tell you that in the eyes of God,
there is really no difference.
The pain and anguish inflicted upon a
human or a being of the animal kingdom is
literally the same.
The cosmic accountability is
also the same because,
"We are All One!"**

There is so much more I would like to talk about, but Louise feels I should limit myself at this time. I have mentioned nothing yet of the abuse of animals in rodeos that so many of you enjoy, not fully knowing what goes on behind the scenes.

RODEOS!
ANIMAL CRUELTY FOR A BUCK!

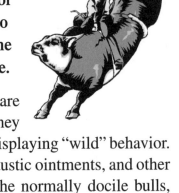

For the animals who suffer broken bones and torn ligaments, broken backs, or burned testicles, the rodeo is just a cruel detour on the way to the slaughterhouse.

Animals used in rodeos are not aggressive by nature. They are physically provoked into displaying "wild" behavior. Electric prods, sharp sticks, caustic ointments, and other painful devices are used on the normally docile bulls, calves, and horses. All animals, including farm and ranch animals, bulls and calves, are feeling beings who experience pain and fear like cats and dogs do—just like humans.

They have not volunteered for those unrefined "entertaining" games. They are helpless victims of humans' insensitivity and heartlessness.

Animals in Zoos and the Circus

What about the zoo keepers who keep animals imprisoned in small cages all of their lives? Did these animals volunteer for this sort of inappropriate lifestyle, or are they kept in captivity against their intent and will? Many have to be sedated to keep them from thrashing in anguish against the bars of their lifelong prison.

What about the circus animals who are dragged from place to place in cages too small for them, who endure too many long hours on the road, being driven from town to town, in the most uncomfortable conditions?

Circus animals live for the sake of profit in the pockets of their captors. No consideration is ever given to their well-being or feelings.

Many of these great animals are grossly abused and mistreated. They are considered *"just commodities"* by the people who think they have a right to own them.

In a society of people who would like to consider themselves "civilized," "enlightened," or "advanced," there should now be an urgent call for the use of animals to be prohibited in circuses and rodeos.

Animals belong in nature, where there are trees and green grass, not in cages or filthy feeding corrals. Do you think circus life provides lions, tigers and elephants the natural environment they need to live a happy life?

If you know anything about the life and fate of circus animals, you would never buy tickets for circus shows that use animals in this entertainment business.

By doing so, you are contributing to the suffering and unnatural lifestyle of these precious animals.

Cruelty in any form is never entertaining for the "enlightened."

Chapter Five

Let My People of the Animal Kingdom Go!

Angelo

I GAVE THE MAIN PART OF MY MESSAGE to Aurelia Louise in 1996. She put it in her computer but now, in 1999, we are finishing this project. Before we close, it is my desire to inform you on one more important issue.

Most people know from the various sacred books and prophesies and many other sources on this planet, that the year 2000 will be the beginning of major changes on the planet and within the human civilizations living here. If you take a look at your sacred books again, and read the various prophecies that have been made regarding the end of this earthly cycle, you will quickly come to realize that all of you, in your hearts, know that major changes are at hand for Earth and her people. These changes are upon us and will begin to manifest tangibly very soon.

These changes will be much more profound than anything a computer virus can create. Most humans are in denial over this great happening, and chose to ignore it. You continue to live your lives on Earth as if you expect to go on forever without any changes.

Angelo says... Not so!

It is not up to me, Angelo, to tell you what will soon transpire on this planet. However, it is my understanding that there will be many different scenarios emerging at different locations on Earth at different times. I can report one event that will happen for sure. Hang on to your boots...

**The time is very, very soon
approaching when, many, many
species of animals who live on
Earth at this time will leave the planet.
As a matter of fact, many species have
already left, and many new species have
already emerged.**

For those who are scheduled to leave and are still here, they are now in the last stages of their preparation. There is nothing that you can do to stop them, no matter who you are or how much you try. The mandate for these animals to leave the Earth has been decreed by the Godhead. Their cycle here is completed.

Their hierarchies have negotiated their return to their home planets and their requests have been granted. They need to leave for their own healing. When the appropriate time draws near, they will be assisted in their departure.

There are others who are scheduled to stay, but will soon begin to mutate into other forms. For example, chickens will mutate into a new species of birds. The cows will mutate into a new species that will be similar to the deer family. In a matter of years, no one will eat anyone else. In the new world, it will be considered a barbaric and shameful practice. All animals and humans will become vegetarians.

Great change is coming to this planet. All animals who have become fearful of mankind or are not friendly towards humanity, those who are afflicted by aggression or hostility, are now preparing to leave. Some species will leave together in groups all at once, and others will be leaving in stages. They have served and fulfilled their purposes on this planet as well as they have been allowed to. The migration process has already begun.

They will be replaced by others of their own species who will be better adapted to the new world we are moving into, or they will be replaced by altogether new species. All aggression in animals will eventually disappear, including the big cats. Their replacements will be as gentle and cooperative as any domestic pussy cat.

People who have a genuine love-bond with a specific animal, such as a cat, a dog or a horse, will be allowed to remain together. They will move into the higher frequency of the New Earth vibration that is about to grace this planet. In the radiance of the New Earth, the little ones, whom you love so much, will be raised into a higher vibration that will enable them, if it is their choice, to stay with you much longer than they do now. Their life span will be extended.

All species of animals have their own planet of origin, and many will be going home.

They are going home to heal and be, once again, in a place where each one will be loved profoundly and unconditionally. They are going where they no longer have to live in constant fear of being attacked, eaten, caged, captured, hunted, abused, or killed. They are going where the "laws of the jungle" or the "survival of the fittest" do not exist. They are going back, each one, to their own planet of origin where only Love exists. They need to heal from the aggression and fear they have taken on by living many thousands, and for some, millions of years on this planet.

All species were very loving and gentle when they first arrived here. All animals and humans were great friends and communicated with each other just as easily as you do now. They have gradually taken into their bodies and souls the aggressive ways of mankind. For thousands of years, by doing so, they have rendered the Earth a great service. They have assisted you with your own personal evolution. Their full healing may take some time, but they are going to a place of great Love and Light where they will be nurtured back to balance and wholeness.

**It is now time for them to
receive their just reward!
In your heart, let them go!**

"Let my People Go," says Angelo!

I can almost feel a level of panic in the emotions of some of you. You are wondering what the Earth is going to be like without certain animals. Know, dear ones, that the Earth will not be without animals. The animals are the Children of the Earth Mother, and she is already prepared to host many new, beautiful and intelligent species that will bring you much delight. She will host them with great love and tenderness. In your heart, will you prepare yourself to do the same?

**Angelo will now reveal the
biggest and best-kept secret
on this planet...**

I am now going to share with you the biggest and best-kept secret on this planet. Aurelia Louise has known this secret for some time, and she is as excited to share it with all of you as I am. We both feel the time has finally come to let this big "cat" out of the bag. Only a few people living on the surface of the planet already know this big secret. Those who read my message will be among the first ones to find out.

Inside the Earth, there are various kinds of civilizations of "immortal" humans. Some of them have been there for a few thousand years, while others have been there as long as one to two hundred thousand years. Some live in the Inner Earth, others live in the Middle Earth, and many more live in the numerous subterranean cities located throughout the Hollow Earth. The people belonging to these civilizations live anywhere between a few hundred years to several thousand years, according to their personal choice. They have third-dimensional bodies like yours, but they are not subject to the same limitations you presently are. For thousands of years, they have lived through the concepts of Love and benevolent Brotherhood. They have attained a very high level of evolution. It makes humans on the Earth's surface seem like children.

They are compassionate and kind and do not judge you. They have very advanced technology compared to you on the surface, which they use for positive purposes only. They are looking forward to emerging soon from their underground paradise. It is their intention to assist all of you in making the transition to the New Earth soon to usher our present reality into a glorious golden age of enlightenment and peace.

**Spiritual preparation is the most
important gift that you can offer
to yourself at this time.**

For example, the Telosians, who are nearly seven-foot-tall humans living in the city of Telos, the subterranean city under Mt. Shasta, California, have been living there for 12,000 years. They went underground when the continent of Lemuria sank into the Pacific Ocean. Because they moved there quite "recently" compared to the length of time other civilizations have been underground, they are considered the "new kids on the block." For surface dwellers, 12,000 years seems to be a very long time, but for Inner Earth civilizations who have been there for so much longer, it is considered quite recent.

It is now time for all of you to expand your consciousness. Most of you have no conception of the long history of your planet. Your historians are aware of only a small fragment of Earth's history. There are millions of humans who live inside the Earth. Telos is considered a medium sized subterranean city, and is presently hosting one and one-half million Lemurians. Contrary to what you have been led to believe, the Lemurians did not all perish when their continent was destroyed. A remnant of their population escaped inside.

the Earth, and are still living there today in the numerous underground cities they have built.

Soon, the underground civilizations are planning to emerge onto the surface once again, after thousands of years of no communication with surface dwellers. At the moment, many of them are in the process of finalizing their preparations for this great event, their emergence to the surface. It will probably not happen in the year 2000, but will, for sure, happen.

The Lemurians have kept intact their ancient culture. They have also evolved to a very high level. If you want to know more about this subject, read the material and messages from the subterranean cities. I now want to continue with my original subject. I don't want to sidetrack.

The Biggest Secret!

Hundreds of animal species who used to be on the surface of this planet thousands of years ago, who are considered "extinct" by your scientists and historians, have never really left the Earth. They have only left the surface. Most of those species are still here, living inside the Earth.

Some animals of almost every species have been safeguarded by various subterranean civilizations during eras when turmoil, wars and fighting were prevalent on the surface. When they moved underground, they took their animals with them. These animals are waiting to emerge onto the surface once again. Their original beauty, intelligence and gentleness have been preserved.

These animals are more perfect than those we have here now, because they have been loved and never abused in any way by the subterranean dwellers. The animal species of the present time, living on the surface, have deteriorated due to the negativity imposed on them. There is a large number of breeds and species you are not yet consciously aware of. Their emergence onto the surface will bring much delight in your future lives. It is so wondrous! Welcome them back in your heart!

When violence between humans and towards the animal kingdom comes to an end, and Inner Earth beings feel their animals will be safe, once again, they will come back to the surface. These magnificent animals will become the new species that will inhabit the New Earth. How exciting! I know that Aurelia Louise can't wait to cuddle up with the big cats again.

Inside the Earth, practically all animals are very friendly and gentle. There are none who have any kind of aggression or fear of humans. They have been handled **only with love** for thousands of years, and they have been treated as younger brothers and sisters. Any aggression within them has been eliminated. All animals are vegetarians inside the Earth; none eat each other. Even the lions and tigers, who are at the top of the food chain on the surface, are docile and vegetarians. Anyone can walk up to them, gently pull their whiskers or their tails and be totally safe. Animals inside the Earth are friendly with humans and communicate telepathically as in ancient times, when darkness and violence did not prevail and all humans on Earth lived by the precepts of Light, Unconditional Love and Brotherhood.

Inside the Earth, the inhabitants live a life of wondrous paradise. They hope you will soon be ready to learn from them how to build a life of paradise for yourself on the surface. When they emerge, they will come as teachers if you are willing to accept them. They hope to offer you a role model which you can duplicate to create a permanent golden age of peace, abundance, love and enlightenment for all on this planet. What a change it will be for us of the animal kingdom!

No one who still harbors in their heart any kind of violence will be allowed to remain within the radiance and wonders of the New Earth. The New Millennium will open the doors to the long-awaited paradise, the return of the Garden of Eden. I would like to suggest that you begin raising your consciousness now if it is your desire to seek admission into this Promised Land. No one will be allowed entrance into this new Garden of Eden if they still carry the negative patterns, lifestyles and vibrations of the old paradigm of violence and fear.

**Inside the Earth is really the place where the lion lies beside the lamb and the little child leads them.
It exists right now as I am speaking! Just a few miles under your feet!**

Angelo's Conclusion

I have much more to share. I would like to tell you about cat heaven and other animal paradises someday; but I have said enough for today. I now need to take my afternoon nap; but I intend to talk to you again another time. Thank you for allowing me to share the burden of my heart with you. Perhaps Aurelia Louise and I will write another book someday. *

The changes that are coming soon to the surface are very positive. Nevertheless, the Earth has to cleanse Herself of the present negativity. Aurelia Louise is preparing us for our safe passage into the New Earth. Do not be afraid.

If you give up your violent and negative ways now, you have nothing to fear. The Inner Earth people will come to assist those who will welcome them into their midst. Their assistance will greatly reduce the various levels of stress that will be produced by the transition.

Editor's note: Writing another book was never to come to pass. Aurelia Louise made her transition in 2009 and Angelo in 2010.

See this time as one of great rejoicing and grand renewal. This time does not represent the ushering out of the end of the world, but the end of the world as we know it.

We are on the threshold of a most wondrous new beginning. Humanity and all of the Earth Kingdoms have been waiting for so very long for this marvelous new age. At last, this time is now upon us. God, along with the assistance of the dedicated spiritual hierarchy of this planet and millions of angels, are now almost ready to deliver the New Earth, perhaps in a twinkle of an eye, by creating a shift of dimension.

This shift of dimension may take a few months to a few years, but we know that it is no longer a matter of decades. The shift has already begun, and it will become clearer and more tangible in the next few years. It is scheduled to be complete by 2012 or perhaps sooner. *

Only those who will resonate with enough love in their hearts will be graced with the privilege of admission into the new paradise. Those who will resist will have to leave the planet or stay behind, in the old world of pain and suffering.

*Editor's note: The Publisher has decided to leave unchanged the author's references to particular dates.

I hope I have touched your heart enough today for you to take my message seriously. I also hope that you will decide to become an activist in protecting us, the "Furry Beings" of the Animal Kingdom.

I thank Aurelia Louise for spending so many hours typing and editing my message on her computer.

It is very urgent that all humans calling themselves Souls of Light, Children of the One, do something about the plight and treatment of animals on this planet.

Aurelia Louise tells us that we are the most precious cats in the whole Universe! Some people might argue with her, but it makes us feel very important and loved.

On behalf of the Animal Kingdom of this planet, Tender-Heart and I send Love, Healing, Hope, and Enlightenment to all. We promise that you will have peace and great abundance when Love is accorded unconditionally to all life forms on our planet. You will find the key to Love in your meditation by exploring the secret chambers of your heart. Go find the true meaning of this word.

And so, Angelo has spoken!

I AM ANGELO, THE ANGEL CAT. I speak on behalf of the evolution of all species of the Animal Kingdom on this planet. I serve on the second cosmic ray of Illumination. I am a teacher. I am assisted by Tender-Heart, the Angel Cat, who serves on the fifth cosmic ray of Healing.

Chapter Six

Message from Adama, The High Priest of Telos

THIS IS ADAMA, THE HIGH PRIEST OF TELOS, the subterranean city under Mt. Shasta. Our friend Aurelia Louise asked me to give a short conclusion to Angelo's message. I consider it my privilege for this opportunity to share some thoughts with all those who will be reading Angelo's important message.

Dear friends, in Telos we have known Angelo for a very long time. Angelo has been an animal companion for Aurelia Louise since the time of Lemuria, when both of them lived in the temples: Aurelia Louise as a high priestess and Angelo as a temple cat. For thousands of years they have graced each other's lives.

The part of Angelo we are more familiar with, is the higher aspect of his soul. In his current little body, he is hosting only a small portion of the totality of his being. Our present encounters with Angelo and Aurelia Louise usually take place in the Inner Planes, at the soul level, when their physical bodies are sleeping. One might say that the Inner Planes are places of Great Encounters. In Telos, we have a much greater conscious awareness of the Inner Planes than you have on the surface, because our DNA coding is more developed.

The message you just read from Angelo comes from the higher aspect of his soul, the part that connects with the Universal Mind. Aurelia Louise recognizes that. As they both connect with the God-Force of the Universal Mind for a specific purpose, great work can be achieved. All of you can do this also. It is only a matter of making a conscious decision to do it, and practicing until you become adept at this process.

We say to you that animals embody again and again, just as you do. Their embodiments are always extensions of a much larger whole. All of us, including the animals, are extensions of a vast Being of Light, so vast and so wondrous that you will stand in absolute wonderment the day you open to the understanding of your true Divinity. It is referred to as the concept of multi-dimensionality, a concept that remains very difficult to fully comprehend by the limitations of a third-dimensional mind.

God is constantly creating and forever extending

and expanding in a wider and wider spectrum of manifestations. The animal kingdom is just one among many of these infinite expansions. All are part of God, dear ones, ALL. When you allow yourself to hurt one part of Life (God) you are hurting the whole, including yourself.

In the Inner Planes, all animals have great intelligence, and are very different than what you could ever imagine in your current awareness. Some of them rule worlds and planets. Animals live in many dimensions. All animals have an over-soul or a higher-self as do humans. They are from a different kingdom than you are, and thus are extensions of a much larger body of consciousness, another aspect of Divinity. Consciousness extends itself from the Highest levels of the Godhead to the lowest level in the first dimension of the rocks and minerals. *All are God in various expressions.*

The higher the dimension, the greater is the understanding of Love and the more expanded the awareness. Animals share your planet with you because, just like you, they have chosen to come here to have a third-dimensional experience. They have also come as helpers and teachers to assist mankind in ways you do not yet understand. Because they chose to come in a body that is different than yours it does not make them inferior to you. There is no moral or spiritual justification for the way many animals are presently treated on the Earth's surface. Their bodies are just an overtone lower than yours in your third-dimensional expression. Let's be clear on that. There is not the difference you have been led to believe and have used as an excuse for animal exploitation.

In your limited understanding, you have allowed yourself to see many species of animals become commodities for selfish means or for profit. We say this is not what or who they are. The golden rule needs to be applied to all sentient beings, not just to the human kingdom. If you wish to move forward on the platform of your own evolution, you can achieve it only by according unconditional love in words, thoughts, feelings and deeds toward all life forms.

Love is the key.

There is no other. There is not one speck of creation that has not been manifested through love. Thus, there is nothing in creation that you can choose "not to love" if you wish to move forward.

In the spirit world, animals function from the fourth- and fifth-dimensional levels. They are all connected to a higher body of Light. All humans are also connected to their own Higher-Selves, referred to as their "I AM Presence" existing in higher dimensions.

The Higher-Self of your being, your own God-Self, is a glorious, intelligent, powerful being of unlimited perfection. Your third-dimensional life on Earth reflects only a small portion of the Divinity you truly are.

In creation and in the Higher Realms, there is no

such thing as lesser, lower, better than, not so good as, etc. These are all labels of limited human awareness. All are equally loved, and considered expressions of God in constant motion (evolution).

There is a difference between you and the animals, but it is not what you have been led to believe. My friends, in the subterranean cities, we have much respect for animals and we consider them as our younger brothers and sisters on the ladder of evolution. We treat them with the same consideration we would like to receive ourselves.

Let's say that in a human family, for example, there are 10 children. Would you say that the younger ones are inferior to the older ones just because they have less life experience and do not yet know as much as the older ones? Would you say that the younger ones do not deserve to be treated with love and consideration, but should be abused because they are not yet as developed as the older ones?

I would think not, because you know very well that in a few years they will catch up. So it is, my friends, with the animals. In the hierarchy or family of the body of the One God, the animals who share our planet are the younger members.

It is my expectation that you will understand the point I am trying to make. Everything in creation has consciousness, from the greatest to the smallest. Ultimately, all are considered equal.

It is accurate information that we have in our care in Telos a large number of species of animals who have been extinct on Earth for a very long time. Other civilizations who have been underground longer than we have, also care for a large number of animal species who have been extinct on the surface much longer. We have many species of cats of all sizes. They vary between five to six pounds to several hundred pounds. We have species of dogs and horses who are more evolved than the ones you know, and who will bring you much delight when they are eventually allowed to emerge among you.

Most of our animals are larger than the ones you now have. For example, many of the big cats are almost twice the size of the ones on the surface. Many horses are larger, and some have retained a size that you will really be able to enjoy.

**Our animals are very dear to us.
Be assured that they will not be
released into your hands until violence
is totally eliminated from your world.**

- All of our animals are gentle and have never been exposed to negativity or violence of any sort. Anyone can walk up to any of them in total safety and cuddle with them.

- None of our animals have any fear of humans, neither do they kill or eat each other. They are all vegetarians.

- Our animals have never been hunted or caged.

They are allowed to live their full lifespan, which is much longer than animals on the surface.

Be assured that we will not take the chance of releasing any of them to the surface civilization as long as there is any possibility for them to be hurt or receive less love than they are accustomed to.

We recognize the unique intelligence each species of animal has, and we have no need to ever bring them into any level of submission. They are docile and willing to please. Telepathic communication is all that is needed for us to have total cooperation with them.

On behalf of all civilizations of the Earth Within, I say to you that it is with great joy and anticipation that we will watch all of you, our dear brothers and sisters, open your minds and hearts to the animal kingdom and begin to change the way you perceive and treat them.

We send you our Love, our Light and our Friendship. We very much look forward to the time of our emergence onto the surface, to be once again with you, to shake your hands and to teach you what we have learned from living for thousands of years in the vibration of Love, Peace and Brotherhood without war, control, greed, fear, manipulation and endless bureaucracy.

The time is soon at hand for our two civilizations to unite in the spirit of a grand cosmic family after thousands of years of physical separation. When we emerge from our subterranean abodes, through the maze of tunnels leading to every country and city of the planet, it will be a time of great rejoicing for all those who will open their hearts and minds to receive us.

It will be a "deliverance" from your struggles, pains and sorrows. Our intention will be to help you create the kind of life you have been longing for, for so very long.

Together, we will forge a very bright future for all of us, citizens of the New Earth. It will be a win-win situation for all. We are your senior brothers and sisters, and we love you all very dearly.

I Am Adama, your Lemurian Brother.

Let There Be Peace on Earth

Let there be peace on Earth
And let it begin with me.
Let there be peace on Earth
The peace that was
meant to be.
With God as Creator,
A family all are we.
Let us walk with each other
In perfect harmony.
Let peace begin with me;
Let this be the moment now.
With every step I take
Let this be my joyful vow:
To take each moment,
And live each moment,
In peace eternally;
Let there be peace on Earth
And let it begin with me!

– *Jill Jackson and Sy Miller*

Prayer for Animals

BELOVED HEAVENLY FATHER, hear our humble prayers. We are pleading for mercy and protection for our friends  the animals, especially those who are suffering in the hands of the ignorant and the insensitive.

We pray for those animals who are hunted or who are lost. We implore mercy for those who are abandoned, frightened, hungry, or in pain. We pray for all those who have no one to love them.

We also pray for the millions of your little ones who are tortured, day after day, year after year, in ruthless experiments in animal research laboratories. We call for mercy in the name of those animals who are caged and subjected to cruel treatment, until an agonizing death delivers them from their oppressors. We ask that animals, once again, be recognized as our younger brothers and sisters on the ladder of Life.

We also ask for forgiveness, O Lord, for the immense oppression that is imposed on the animal kingdom! Please send your millions of angels to comfort, heal and nurture those unfortunate ones. We plead for Thy mercy and compassion for all animal beings on this planet. And for the aggressors, we ask that you open and soften their hearts.

For those who have the courage to rescue animals and champion their rights, we ask for their protection and the abundance they need to continue their work. We ask that they be blessed beyond measure. Help us understand that all animals, great and small, are part of God's precious creation and part of a greater design, unknown to our human mind.

We are ever so grateful for the beings of the animal kingdom, who have graced our planet with so much love and tolerance. Make us instruments of true friendship with animals and all life forms so that we may share the blessings of the meek and the merciful.

Suggested Reading

Animal Liberation *Peter Singer*
Animal Talk *Penelope Smith*
Animal Rights Handbook *Living Planet Press*
Animal Wisdom *Anita Curtis*
Because They Matter *Cindy Traisi*
Free the Animals *Ingrid Newkirk*
Inhumane Society *Dr. Michael Fox, D.V.M.*
Is This the Place? *Leo Grillo, DELTA Rescue*
Kinship with All Life *J. Allen Boone*
Life Song *Bill Schull*
Stolen for Profit *Judith Reitman*

The Souls of Animals *Gary Kowalski*

Talking with Nature *Michael J. Roads*

Fairies at Work and at Play *Geoffrey Hodson*

The Runaway Fairy *Molly Brett*

The Compassion of Animals *Kristin Von Kreisle*

There Are No Problem Horses,
Only Problem Riders *Mary Twelveponies*

The Call Goes Out: Important Message from the
Earth's Cetaceans *Dianne Robbins*

The Call Goes Out From Telos: Messages from
the Subterranean Cities *Dianne Robbins*

The Voice of the Infinite in the Small *Joanne E. Lauck*

Animal-Speak: Spiritual & Magical Powers of All
Creatures Great and Small *Ted Andrews*

Diet for a New America: How Your Food Choices
Affect Your Health, Happiness and the Future of
Life on Earth *John Robbins*

Of course, dear readers, there are many more wonderful and compassionate books regarding this subject. I am sure there are many new ones I am not familiar with. May the blessings of the Universe shower upon you the wondrous Gifts of Love and Compassion.

Angelo's Mission

Please support Angelo's Mission by ordering your own copy of this book. Help spread this message around the world by ordering extra copies. May we suggest that you buy several copies of this book and sell them or give them to your friends and people in your entourage. Violence towards animals on this planet has to STOP NOW!

If we cannot count on those who are awakened regarding the sad plight of animals for support, I do not know on whom we can count. My friend, you who champions the rights of animals, may we count on you to spread this message to as many people as possible?

A portion of the profit made from the sale of this book will be used to serve the great need for the education that is required to help people open their heart to the understanding of the grave consequences of violence toward any form of life and help restore, through Love, the ethical treatment and rights of animals on this planet.

The Universe is weeping for the plight of animals and is grateful for your contribution as a champion for their legitimate rights to be living on this planet with dignity, equality and respect.

To order more copies of Angelo's Message, please visit our website:

http://mslpublishing.com

Mount Shasta Light Publishing Publications

The Seven Sacred Flames........................$39.00

Prayers to the Seven Sacred Flames.................$7.00

The Ascension Flame of Purification and Immortality....$7.00

Seven Sacred Flames Card Deck $16.00

Telos Book Series Card Deck......................$16.00

Telos – Volume 1 "Revelations of the New Lemuria" ...$18.00

Telos – Volume 2 "Messages for the Enlightenment
of a Humanity in Transformation".................$18.00

Telos – Volume 3 "Protocols of the Fifth Dimension" ...$20.00

The Effects of Recreational Drugs on
Spiritual Development $4.00

Spanish Translations:

Las Siete Llamas Sagradas.......................$24.00

Oraciones de las Siete Llamas Sagradas $7.00

La Llama de le Ascension de Purificacion
e Inmortalidad.................................. $7.00

These publications can be purchased in the USA:
- Directly from us by phone or at our mailing address. If ordering by mail, please call for sales tax and shipping and handling charges and preferences.
- From our secure shopping cart on our web site: **http://www.mslpublishing.com**
- From Amazon.com
- Bookstores through New Leaf Book Distributing

Mount Shasta Light Publishing
P.O. Box 1509
Mount Shasta, CA 96067-1509
info@mslpublishing.com
Phone: (Intl: 001) 530-926-4599 / 530-926-4159 Fax
(If no answer, please leave a message)

Publisher's Note:

AURELIA LOUISE JONES made her transition in July of 2009 and Angelo, the beloved Angel Cat, followed Aurelia Louise in April of 2010. They were devoted companions and no doubt, they are once again together in the other realms. Perhaps Angelo has paid a visit to his planet, Khaath, and a visit to Telos, the Lemurian City of Light, as well. The rest of the Universe is waiting for humans to wake up to Angelo's Message, a vitally important message at this time, raising the awareness of the plight of animals and how they are treated on this planet.